Introduction

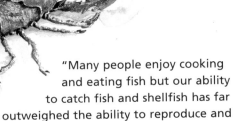

"Many people enjoy cooking and eating fish but our ability to catch fish and shellfish has far outweighed the ability to reproduce and the marine environment as a whole is increasingly under pressure. Careful management of the fish resource as well as the marine environment is a necessity.

Anyone who eats fish and shellfish should think about where they come from, whether they're in season, and how they have been caught. This book aims to promote eating fish and shellfish in a sustainable way.

The book contains a mixture of superb recipes from local chefs as well as plenty of conservation tips. We hope you enjoy it."

Bridget Loveday

" The sea is a wonderful resource for human beings and as fishermen we must start to farm it instead of hunt it, otherwise stocks will become depleted and eventually lost".

David Sales, Local fisherman

Mussel and Sea Beet Gratin

Hugh Fearnley-Whittingstall

Mussels

Seed mussels are taken from the Shambles Bank, off Portland, and grown on in sheltered water. Try to buy local mussels that are grown in a sustainable way rather than ones that have travelled half-way around the world.

Ingredients

500g sea beet
(or fresh leaf spinach)

300ml milk

55g butter

55g plain flour

pinch of nutmeg

2 tbsp grated
parmesan cheese

knob of butter

2 cloves garlic, crushed

A glass of wine

1kg fresh mussels

salt and freshly ground
black pepper

55g fresh white
breadcrumbs

Starter - serves 4
Main meal - serves 2

Method

1. Wash and trim the sea beet. Wilt it in a pan of boiling water

2. When wilted, drain, squeeze dry and chop finely

3. Heat the milk but do not bring to the boil

4. In a separate pan melt the butter, add the flour, cook for a few minutes, then gradually add the hot milk, stirring continuously, to get a smooth, thick béchamel sauce. Stir in the sea beet, nutmeg and half the parmesan

5. In a large pan melt the knob of butter and fry the garlic for 1 minute, add a splash of wine and a little water. When boiling, add the mussels and steam them open (this may take several batches)

6. Remove the mussel meat from their shells, add to the sea beet sauce thinning the mixture with a couple of spoonfuls of mussel cooking liquor. Season with salt and pepper to taste

7. Spread the mixture into an ovenproof shallow dish. Mix the breadcrumbs with some parmesan and sprinkle over the top

8. Bake in the oven at 200°C, 400°F or gas mark 6 for approximately 10 minutes until golden brown

Crustacea Soup Hugh Fearnley-Whittingstall

Method

1. Boil all the crustacea in fresh seawater until cooked (approximately 10 minutes)

2. When cool, remove the brown and white crab meat. Peel the prawns and set the tail meat aside separately from the crab meat

3. Discard the main carapace of the brown crabs. Put the rest of the shells in a bowl and pound with a hammer or rolling pin

4. Heat the oil in a large pan and add the onion, carrot, tomato, garlic, herbs, parsley stalks and leek tops. Fry until soft, add the hammered shells and the fish

5. Pour over enough water to cover, bring to the boil and simmer for 20 minutes

6. Remove the shellfish stock from the heat and either; strain through a heavy-duty conical sieve or put in a heavy-duty blender, whizz up and pass through a sieve

7. Place the sieved liquid in a clean pan over a low heat, stir in the meat from the crabs and season to taste with black pepper, cayenne and salt

8. Heat through but do not boil

To serve: place in warm bowls adding the meat from the prawns.

Ingredients

1 large or 2 medium brown crabs or spider crabs

12 velvet crabs and/or shore crabs

225g local prawns

2 hermit crabs (optional)

1 onion, chopped

1 carrot, chopped

1 large or 2 small tomatoes, chopped

4 cloves of garlic, crushed

a few sprigs of wild fennel (optional)

a few sprigs of wild chervil (optional)

parsley stalks (optional)

leek tops (optional)

1 whole fresh white fish, such as plaice or wrasse (optional)

pinch of cayenne pepper

salt and fresh ground black pepper

olive oil

Serves 4

Fillet of Red Mullet on a Bed of Cous-Cous with Basil Pesto

Ingredients

750g red mullet fillet

250g cous-cous

salt and pepper

500ml olive oil

1 red pepper, diced

1 green pepper, diced

1 yellow pepper, diced

2 large bunches basil

100g grated parmesan

1 clove garlic

1 handful pine kernels

Serves 4

Sustainability

Sustainable fishing means that although fishermen remove fish from the sea, the numbers of fish are kept at a healthy level so that future generations can enjoy this resource.

Method

1. Remove scales from the red mullet and fillet fish (take care to remove pin bones). Place fish (skin up) on a hot, oiled grill tray covered in foil

2. Oil fillets and season with sea salt. Place under a high temperature grill for 4 to 8 minutes depending on the thickness of the fillet

3. Place cous-cous in a bowl with salt, pepper and olive oil, stir. Add water to moisten, stir. Cover bowl with cling film and place in a microwave on high for 2 - 4 minutes

4. When cooked add diced mixed peppers and serve warm

5. Place the basil, parmesan, garlic, pine kernels, olive oil, salt and pepper in a food processor and puree

To serve: place the warm cous-cous in the centre of a plate with the red mullet fillets on top. Spoon the pesto around the cous-cous and serve.

Janet and Arthur Watson

Riverside Restaurant & Seafood Bar

West Bay Bridport

DT6 4EZ

Tel: 01308 422011

Rosemary Baked Cod with a Dressing of Capers and Olive Oil

Riverside Restaurant

Dorset Cod

Dorset Cod is in short supply and stocks are dwindling here and around the UK- as an alternative try Whiting.

Method

1. Lightly butter a baking tray and place a sprig of rosemary on it. Put the cod fillet on top of the rosemary
2. Butter and season the fish and place it into a hot oven for 8 - 10 minutes until the fish is cooked
3. In a small pan put three parts of good quality olive oil to one part good balsamic vinegar, salt and pepper, together with some small capers and thinly sliced sun dried tomatoes
4. Gently warm for 10 minutes, stir but do not boil

To serve: place cod onto a hot plate, spoon a coating of the dressing all over and finish with a sprig of rosemary. Serve with new potatoes and a salad.

Ingredients

1kg cod fillet

knob of butter

4 large sprigs of rosemary

150ml olive oil

50ml balsamic vinegar

salt and pepper

25g capers

25g sliced sun-dried tomatoes

Serves 4

Fillet of Brill with Crispy Spinach and Sorrel Sauce

Riverside Restaurant

Ingredients

4 fillets brill

unsalted butter

450g spinach

6 shallots (chopped)

caster sugar and ginger if desired

dry white wine

white wine vinegar

500ml double cream

2 bunches sorrel

salt and pepper

Serves 4

Method

1. Place fillets (skin side down) on pre-warmed foil. Brush with butter and season with salt and pepper

2. Cook on a high heat for 2 - 8 minutes depending on its thickness

3. Wash and de-stalk the spinach. Roll into a tight cylinder shape and chop thinly with a sharp knife. Put into a deep fryer at 380°F and shake until it becomes crispy. Place on absorbent kitchen paper and keep warm

4. Place the shallots in a pan, cover with dry white wine and reduce over a low heat until it is nearly all gone. Add a splash of white wine vinegar and reduce again

5. Add double cream and bring to the boil, take off the heat and add the sorrel. Puree the mixture and check the seasoning

To serve: place the brill fillets on a warm plate, spoon the warm sorrel sauce around them and a quantity of crispy spinach on the side.

Brill is a marvellously versatile fish. It has a delicate flavour and is found in good supply in Dorset waters. It is a wonderful fish caught off the West Dorset coast, previously disregarded as inferior to Turbot but now much desired.

Hot Dorset Shellfish with Spicy Tomato

Riverside Restaurant

The sea is an ever changing, fragile environment.

Damage to the seabed, pollutants and the loss of species can have a detrimental effect on the future of one of our most precious natural resources.

Method

1. Fry onions and garlic in a large saucepan with some olive oil for 8 minutes
2. Add diced peppers and pulped tomato together with a good pinch of mixed herbs. Leave to reduce gently for 2 - 3 hours or until it reaches a good thick consistency
3. Place a couple of large spoonfuls of the spicy tomato mixture into a large shallow pan. Add a good splash of dry white wine, olive oil and add a pinch of dried chilli flakes
4. Add your choice of shellfish. This could be already cooked and cracked crab, lobster, prawns, langoustines, scallops in their shell, open oysters, clams or mussels
5. Place a tight-fitting lid on the pan and cook for 5-10 minutes depending on the quantity, and shake hard at least twice

Serve steaming in a large soup plate or bowl.

Ingredients

1 medium onion

1 clove garlic

olive oil

2 diced peppers (red and yellow)

1 tin chopped tomatoes

mixed herbs

dry white wine

dried chilli flakes

your choice of shellfish

Serves 2

Ingredients

6 scallops - dive picked

dessert spoon garlic butter

50g mushrooms

1 tbsp double cream

black pepper

dessert spoon white wine

5g chopped fresh parsley

Serves: 6 scallops for a main meal, 3 for a starter

Lyme Bay Scallops

Marsh Barn Restaurant

Method

1. Prepare the scallops by opening them up and carefully cleaning them, retaining the liquid if possible

2. Melt the garlic butter in a small, heavy bottomed frying pan. Add the mushrooms and fry gently until soft

3. Add the scallops and simmer gently for a minute on both sides

4. Add the seasoning, cream and white wine. Simmer to reduce the sauce for 1 minute

To serve: add the parsley and serve in a scallop shell with granary bread and a side salad.

West Bay Crab Paté

David and Gill Sales
Marsh Barn Restaurant
Burton Road
Bridport DT6 4PS
Tel: 01308 422755

Method

1. Melt butter in a heavy saucepan, add the crabmeat and warm

2. Stir in the lightly beaten egg yolk, double cream and lemon juice until the mixture thickens slightly

3. Pack tightly into small ramekin dishes and allow to cool

4. Seal the top with melted butter

Serve with hot toast and lemon slices.

Ingredients

225g fresh cooked crab meat, $1/2$ white, $1/2$ brown

1 egg yolk

50g salted butter

1 tbsp double cream

black pepper

cayenne

lemon juice

Serves 4 -5

Conservation Tip

Choose diver collected scallops because:

It is a better way of harvesting

There is no disturbance to the seabed

It is a better product because the scallops are undamaged and clean

David Sales - West Bay lobster potter

David Sales has fished Dorset waters since 1957. During this time he has seen many changes within the fishing industry.

"Once this was a community made up of generations of traditional local families working with nature. Now there are few families left in the business and more commercial enterprises have taken their place. The biggest change came during the early 1960s when almost overnight the fishing industry was converted from a local cottage industry to a larger commercial industry.

Small boats, using fishing gear made from natural fibre, changed to using new strong synthetic fibres, which, enabled bigger boats to be used. With everything increasing in size and strength, inevitably the amount of fish being caught rapidly increased. Adding to this change there was the development of technology and where once fishermen relied on landmarks, maps and compass they now have more accurate navigation equipment using satellite systems."

Fishermen today can fish exact locations, sometimes until stocks become threatened.

Nets

Nets set near nesting bird colonies may result in birds becoming entangled and drowned.

Smoked Haddock on a Rosti with Hollandaise Sauce and Crispy Leeks

Floods Bistro

Ingredients

1 medium sized potato

oil

2 inch piece of leek

milk

200g smoked haddock

2 tbsp lemon juice

2 tbsp white wine vinegar

12 peppercorns

2 egg yolks

100g unsalted butter

Serves 2

Method

1. Peel and grate potato. Squeeze the starch out and dry with kitchen towel
2. Heat oil in a frying pan and add the potato, turning frequently until it is golden brown
3. Cut the leeks into two inch strips and deep fry until golden brown
4. Place smoked haddock in a pan and cover with milk and gently boil for about 4 - 5 minutes

Hollandaise Sauce

1. Boil the white wine vinegar, lemon juice and peppercorns and reduce to 1 tablespoon of liquid
2. Strain and allow to cool
3. In a pan add the eggs and half the butter to the liquid
4. On a very low heat add the rest of the butter gradually whisking vigorously
5. Remove from the heat and whisk until the liquid has the texture of double cream

To serve: place rosti (potato) on a plate with the fish on top, cover with hollandaise sauce and the leeks and serve.

Grilled Dover Sole with Caper and Parsley Butter

Tom Flood

Floods Bistro
19 Custom House Quay
Weymouth
Telephone 01305 772270

Method

1. Remove the dark skin from the fish
2. Cover with plain flour and season with salt and pepper
3. Brush both sides of the fish with butter and place on a tray
4. Cook under a grill on a medium heat until golden brown
5. In a pan heat the unsalted butter, capers and parsley until it is nut brown in colour

To serve: place the fish on a warm plate and pour over the caper and parsley sauce.

Ingredients

50g unsalted butter

lemon juice

2 dover sole

plain flour

1 tbsp capers

salt and pepper

1 tbsp chopped parsley

Serves 2

Eat seasonally and locally

It is important to remember that not all fish are available at all times of the year so eat fish that are in season, they will be locally caught and therefore fresher and better tasting. Plaice and Dover Sole are best in spring, Bass in summer, Lemon Sole in winter while crabs are best outside the summer season.

3 Crab Soup

Mr and Mrs Miles

Storm Fish Restaurant

16 High St,
Poole
BH15 1BP

Telephone:
01202 674970

Ingredients

100g leeks

125g butter

100g carrot (finely chopped)

100g onion (finely chopped)

3 bay leaves

sprig of thyme

10g parsley stalks

50ml cream

50ml brandy

cayenne pepper

500g brown crab

500g velvet crab

500g spider crab

2½ tbsp tomato puree

200ml white wine

2 litres fish stock

Serves 6

Method

1. Melt 100g butter in a deep pan and add the carrot, onion, leek, bay leaf, thyme and parsley stalks

2. Cook to a light brown colour

3. Prepare the crabs by removing the shells, wash the crabs, split the crab in half and discard the sac

4. Add the pieces to the pan and season with salt and pepper. Fry until the crab turns red on all sides and then pour half the brandy over the crab and flambé

5. Add the tomato puree, white wine and fish stock and bring to the boil. Season lightly and simmer gently for 20 minutes

6. Pound the flesh and the shells of the crabs and return to the soup, simmer gently for 30 minutes diluting with a little water if necessary

7. Pass through a fine strainer into a clean pan. Re-boil the soup adding the cream, the remainder of the butter, the rest of the brandy and a little cayenne

Serve in a large bowl with garlic and rosemary croutons.

The size limit of crabs and lobsters before they can be landed has increased, bringing them up to international standards. Currently the minimum landing sizes are:

Species	Size(mm)
Brown crab	140
Female spider crab	120
Male spider crab	130
Velvet crab	65
Lobster	87

Specialities of Dorset

Certain species are Dorset specialities, and are
currently thought to be in plentiful supply.
These include Spider crabs and Mackerel.

Ingredients

12 scallops, cleaned

12 scallop shells

4 cloves of garlic

$\frac{1}{2}$ tsp of chopped chilli

100g smoked bacon lardons

1 bunch spring onions, with the green parts chopped

170ml olive oil

1 bunch watercress

Serves 4

Seared Dived Scallops with Bacon, Chilli, Garlic and Scallions

Mallams at the Quay Restaurant

Method

1. Heat the oil in a heavy pan. Add the bacon lardons and cook until they are just beginning to crisp. Add the garlic and the chopped chilli

2. Heat a searing dish and sear the scallops for only 1 - 2 minutes each side

3. Place the scallops into the olive oil mix. Add the spring onion tops to soften

To serve: place a small amount of the bacon into each of the warmed scallop shells. Top with a scallop and spoon the remaining olive oil mix into the shells. Place three scallop shells on a plate and garnish with a small bunch of watercress.

Roast Sea Bass on Tempura Vegetables with Seared Scallops and a Saffron Sauce

Method

1. Clean the scallops
2. Sear the sea bass on a branding plate skin side down, put aside
3. Roast the fish in a hot oven for 8 -10 minutes
4. Sear scallops in a small frying pan for 1 - 2 minutes each side

The batter:
5. Whisk the eggs and iced water. Add the flour and bicarbonate of soda, mix briskly with a knife, the batter should be slightly lumpy
6. Dip the vegetables and the coral in the batter and drop into hot oil (200°C) in small batches until golden. Drain on absorbent paper and keep warm

The sauce:
7. Place the wine and saffron into small pan and reduce by a third
8. Add fish stock and cream, bring to the boil and then simmer to thicken

To serve: put a small selection of the vegetables in the centre of a warm plate and arrange three scallops around the edge. Place a bass fillet on top of the vegetables and spoon saffron sauce between the scallops.

Stephen Gosson
Mallams at the Quay
Restaurant
5 Trinity Street
Weymouth
DT4 8TJ
Tel: 01305 777150

Ingredients

4 100g centre cut fillet of sea bass

12 scallops (dive picked not dredged)

For the Batter
4 eggs

225ml iced water

125g sifted plain flour

pinch of bicarbonate of soda

Selection of vegetables to dip in the batter:
batons of carrot

fine beans

broccoli florets

slices of fennel bulb

baby asparagus

rounds of courgette

For the sauce
85ml dry white wine

55ml fish stock

140ml cream

saffron threads

Serves 4

Local inshore fishermen

Fishermen start their day in the early hours of the morning. The smaller inshore boats are restricted by the weather but the more powerful, bigger boats can venture out in all kinds of weather and further offshore so can fish all year round.
This threatens certain fish stocks which traditionally had a resting period during bad weather.

Gratin of White Crab Meat

Method

1. Place the white wine, garlic and shallots in a pan and reduce to a syrup consistency
2. Add the brandy, remove from the heat and allow to cool
3. Whisk the eggs and the double cream together
4. Add the shallot mixture, cheese, crabmeat and the seasonings. Pour into a buttered 8cm mould and steam until firm (approximately 45 minutes)
5. Prepare the sauce by putting the fish stock, wine and cream in a pan and reducing by two thirds. Remove from the heat and add the egg yolks, butter, 30g of the cheese and the whipped cream

To serve: place a little warmed buttered spinach leaf on a plate. Turn out the cooked crab from the mould and cover with the sauce. Sprinkle on remaining parmesan and glaze under a hot grill until golden brown. Serve with steamed new potatoes.

Ingredients

For the crab mix:

20g finely chopped shallots

50ml dry white wine

chopped garlic

2 eggs

75g grated cheddar cheese

340g picked white crab meat

20ml brandy

30ml double cream

lemon juice, black pepper, tabasco and English mustard

For the sauce:

600ml fish stock

150ml dry white wine

300ml double cream

2 egg yolks

30g butter

100ml whipped cream

60g parmesan cheese

Serves 4

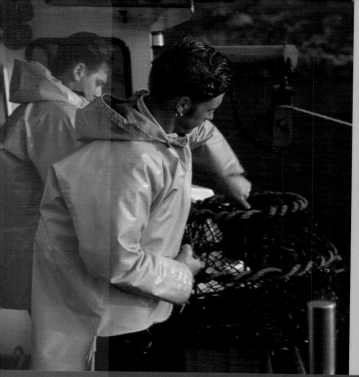

Where to find local fish

There are still fish shops in Dorset that have a wonderful selection of local fresh fish. Much of the fish has been landed that same day and many will give advice on how to cook or prepare the different types.

Local Fishermen will sell their catch to you when they come in to harbour; all you need to do is ask - just be on the quay when the boats are due in and you are bound to walk away with something tasty!

Ingredients

Onion bhajis

150g red onions

25ml cold water

juice of $1/4$ small lemon

$1/2$ egg

75g chickpea flour

1 tsp cumin seeds

1 tsp turmeric

1 desert spoon chilli oil

6 small cod fillets (skin left on)

15g seasoned flour

1 tsp each of ground coriander, paprika, cumin and $1/2$ tsp ginger

Ragôut of chickpea

1 tsp ghee

1 onion (finely chopped)

1 glove of garlic (chopped)

chopped fresh chilli

6 spring onions

10g grated root ginger

2 tsp ground coriander

1 tsp ground cumin

1 tsp turmeric

110g chickpeas (soaked overnight)

150g prepared plum tomatoes (blanched, skinned and chopped)

chopped fresh coriander

125g chopped leaf spinach cooked to yield approximately 25g

Serves 6

Method

To make the bhajis

1. Mix together the cold water, egg and lemon juice. Add the remaining dry ingredients and mix to a batter. Allow to stand for 15 minutes
2. Add the sliced red onions and mix well. Shape into small balls and fry in vegetable oil at 165°C. Allow three bhajis for each piece of cod

To make the Ragôut of chickpea

3. Fry the onion in the ghee. Add the garlic, ginger and a little chopped chilli. Add the rest of the spices mixing well. Put in the oven for 5 minutes at 180°C, 350°F or gas mark 4
4. Stir in the chickpeas, cooked spinach, tomatoes and coriander

To complete the dish:

5. Coat the cod in the seasoned flour. Place skin down in a pan of hot chilli oil and fry until crisp. Turn skin side up and finish cooking in a hot oven

To serve: place the chickpea ragôut onto a warm plate and add the cooked cod and onion bhajis. Garnish with lambs lettuce, leaf coriander and small amounts of chilli oil.

Perrys
Restaurant
4 Trinity Road
The Old Harbour
Weymouth
DT4 8TJ
Tel: 01305 785799

Roast Fillet of Cod with Onion Bhajis and Ragôut of Chickpea

Fillet of Plaice Charmouth

Ingredients

2 x 500g plaice filleted

25g chopped shallots

85ml dry vermouth

2 tomatoes

100g sliced mushrooms

100g mussels (cooked - reserve liquid)

150ml lobster sauce or lobster soup

2 tbsp double cream

chopped parsley

seasoning

Serves 2

Method

1. Place the shallots and mushrooms in an earthenware dish

2. Place the fish into the dish, season and add the vermouth with some of the cooking liquor from the mussels. Cover with buttered paper and poach gently in a moderate oven 175°C , 350°F gas mark 4 for 5 - 10 minutes

3. To prepare the sauce, peel the tomatoes (place in boiling water for a few minutes), remove the seeds and dice them

4. Put the lobster sauce into a pan and bring to the boil. Add the cooking liquor, shallots, mushrooms, mussels, tomato, parsley and cream. Season to taste and bring to the boil

To serve: place fish on a plate and cover with the sauce.

Mr Russel Porter

The Polly Victoria

15 Marine Parade

Lyme Regis

DT7 3JF

Telephone 01294 442886

Plaice

Try Flounder instead of Plaice. It is in plentiful supply in Dorset and tastes good too!

Spicy Caribbean Cod

Peter Bowkett

Method

1. Add oil to a frying pan and fry onions until soft
2. Add the garlic and all the spices with the sugar and salt. Stir and cook for 1 minute
3. Add the juice from the pineapples, tomatoes and tomato puree. Bring to the boil, stirring all the time, and gently simmer uncovered for 10 minutes
4. Stir in the cod and pineapple pieces and simmer until the cod is cooked

To make it a little more exotic you could add some prawns

No Take Zones:

These are areas that are temporarily or permanently closed to fishing and other exploitative activity. They can provide long term benefits to conservationists and to fishermen as the seabed habitats remain undisturbed, providing 'safe' places where fish and other marine species can live. They provide a supply of fish which move away into fished waters.

Ingredients

2 tbsp oil

450g cod, skinned and cubed

200g tinned pineapple pieces in their juice

1 onion, finely chopped

2 cloves of garlic, finely chopped

350g tinned chopped tomatoes

2 tbsp tomato puree

2 tsp masala

1 tsp ground ginger

1 tsp all spice

$\frac{1}{4}$ tsp cayenne

1 tsp sugar

$\frac{1}{2}$ tsp salt

Serves 2

6 Abbotsbury Oysters

ABBOTSBURY OYSTERS

Mr M. Rodwell

Abbotsbury Oysters
Seafood Bar
Ferry Bridge, Weymouth
DT4 9YU

Tel: 01305 788867

Conservation Tip

Regulations and closed seasons: Regulations to prohibit fishing, in certain areas at different times of the year work well as they allow spawning areas to be protected, thus enabling fish populations to be replenished.

Species	Area	Dates of restriction
Cockles	Throughout Dorset	1st Feb - 30th April
Oysters	Throughout Dorset	1st March - 30th Oct
Prawns	Poole Harbour	1st Jan - 31st July
Winkles	Throughout Dorset	15th May - 15th Sept
Clams	Poole Harbour	By licence only

Ingredients

6 'Abbotsbury oysters'

2 finely chopped shallots

$\frac{1}{2}$ cup of sparkling wine

1 large tomato

Juice of $\frac{1}{2}$ a lemon

Method

1. Heat the wine in a saucepan
2. Add the finely chopped shallots and tomato to the wine, cook for 40 seconds
3. Add the oyster meat and lemon juice and cook for a further 30 seconds

To serve: place the oysters and the sauce back into their shells and serve.

Serves: 6 Oysters for a main meal, 3 for a starter

A Trio of Local Oysters

Terry Woolcock
The Sea Cow Restaurant
7 Custom House Quay
Weymouth
DT4 8BE
Tel: 01305 783524

Ingredients

6 'Abbotsbury oysters'

2 shallots

dill, basil and chives

garlic butter

white Burgundy

cream

a sprinkling of Gruyere cheese

mixed herbs

1 tsp sun dried tomato butter

1 tsp garam marsala butter

wholemeal bread

1 lemon

Method

1. Open the oysters and leave them on the half shell
2. Prepare 2 oysters with each of the following mixtures

- Put onto oyster a mix of finely chopped shallot, dill, basil, chive and garlic butter. Add a little Burgundy, cream and a sprinkling of Gruyere cheese
- Put onto oyster finely chopped shallot and mixed herbs. Add the sun dried tomato butter
- Put onto oyster finely chopped shallot and mixed herbs. Add the garam marsala butter and some cream

3. Grill the oysters lightly (too long will toughen them)

*To serve: arrange on a plate and
serve with some wholemeal bread and lemon.*

Serves: 6 Oysters for a main meal, 3 for a starter

Conservation Tip

If you don't want the fish or shellfish you have caught then put it back into the sea immediately. Fish that are returned to the sea straight away have a far better chance of survival.

Ingredients

250g monkfish

100g samphire

285ml of seafood sauce (prepared from fish trimmings and shellfish)

2 tbsp créme fraiche

olive oil

garlic butter

lemon juice

chopped herbs

sea salt

1 dessert spoon chopped shallots and onions

1 dessert spoon Chardonnay

1 dessert spoon Cognac

Serves 2

Monkfish served on a Rich Seafood Sauce with Samphire (sea asparagus)

Method

1. Cut monkfish into collops (slices)
2. Lightly pan fry the monkfish on both sides in olive oil and garlic butter. Add the lemon juice, herbs and season with sea salt. Remove and keep warm
3. In the same pan sauté the samphire so it stays bright green. Remove and keep warm
4. In the same pan add the shallots, onions, herbs, Chardonnay, 4 tbsp of seafood sauce and the Cognac
5. Bring to the boil and reduce until the sauce begins to thicken, bring away from the heat and stir in the créme fraiche (do not re-boil - as sauce may separate)

To serve: run some sauce onto the middle of each plate. Add some samphire and place 6 pieces of monkfish in a circle on top. Dress with shredded deep fried caramelised vegetables (leek, fennel and celeriac are good with fish). Flash under the grill and serve warm to enhance the flavours.

Terry Woolcock

The Sea Cow Restaurant

7 Custom House Quay

Weymouth

DT4 8BE

Tel: 01305 783524

Lobster Lady Tweedsmuir

The Sea Cow Restaurant

Method

1. Boil the lobster gently
2. Cut in half down the centre of the back and remove all the meat from the body and the claws, trying to reserve the claw meat as whole. Cut the body meat into small collops (slices)
3. Heat butter in a shallow pan add the pieces of lobster meat, finely chopped shallots and half the herbs. Set aside in a separate bowl and keep warm
4. To the same pan add the shellfish stock, lemon juice and the Burgundy. Reduce this right down until there is only a small amount of sticky concentrate remaining. Add the Drambuie and continue to reduce. Stir in the double cream
5. Add the remaining herbs and all of the lobster to the sauce and warm

To serve: dress the lobster meat into the two warm $1/2$ lobster shells and spoon the sauce over. Grill very lightly to glaze.

Serves 2

Ingredients

1 whole 400g lobster

$1^1/_2$ tbsp lemon juice

150ml shellfish stock

55ml white Burgundy

150ml double cream

55ml Drambuie

juice from $1/_4$ of a lime

chopped dill and basil

25g shallots

V-notching

V-notching lobsters is just one technique that contributes to fisheries conservation. It has been adopted throughout Britain including the Dorset coast.
The technique involves undersized lobsters having a small v-shaped notch cut from the back section of their tail.
It then becomes illegal to land these lobsters and any caught are returned immediately to the sea. The notch eventually grows out by which time the lobsters have had a chance to breed at least twice. Therefore keeping the lobsters at a sustainable level.

Pan-fried Razor Clams with Pancetta Ham and Roasted Sweet Peppers Hamiltons

Ingredients

3 - 4 large razor clams per person

150g pancetta ham cut into thin strips

2 large red peppers

50g flat leaf parsley chopped coarse

50g unsalted butter

sunflower oil

Serves 4

Method

1. Cut the peppers in half lengthways and remove the seeds. Rub with oil, place on a greased baking sheet and roast in a hot oven for 15 - 20 minutes until the skin comes away from the flesh

2. When cool remove the skins and cut the flesh into strips

3. Scrub the razor clams shells in running cold water to remove any debris

4. Place clams in a large heavy-bottomed pan with enough cold water to cover the bottom of the pan. Cover with a tight fitting lid and place on a high heat, shaking the pan occasionally to keep the clams turning over. Keep turning them until they are all open then drain into a colander and remove them from their shells (keeping the shells)

5. Remove the blackish sac from the cooked clams using your finger. Wash the cooked clams

6. Add two tablespoons of oil to a hot frying pan and fry the pancetta ham for 2 - 3 minutes. Add the clams and heat for 3 - 4 minutes. Finally add the peppers, heat again and add the butter and parsley

Serve on warm plates using the shells for decoration.

Fishermans tale

A good sprat year often means there could be increased numbers of seabirds which feed on the sprats. They also attract shoals of other fish such as bass and herring.

Scallop aquaculture: Hugh Wiltshire is involved in commercial scallop aquaculture in Portland Harbour. It is a sustainable method of farming scallops and works on a 4-year cycle.

An area of Portland seabed is leased to Hugh who also has to apply for a Several order. This means that the seabed is protected from other commercial ventures, which may disturb it. Other activities, however, can take place on the water, such as windsurfing without causing any detrimental effect.

Pasta Bows with Roasted Cherry Tomatoes, Basil, Olive Oil and Pan-fried Lulworth Scallops

Method

1. Cut the cherry tomatoes in half and place in an earthenware dish. Season with salt, freshly milled pepper and a generous amount of olive oil

2. Roast in a moderate oven for 15 to 20 minutes

3. Cook the pasta in a pan with plenty of boiling salted water

4. Lightly fry the scallops in a pan with oil and butter

5. In a large bowl mix together the drained pasta, the scallops, basil and roasted tomatoes, add more olive oil and season to taste

Serve on warmed pasta bowls with hot ciabatta bread to mop up the tasty juices.

Serves 3 - 4

Ingredients

16 Lulworth scallops, cut from their shells and cleaned

300g cherry tomatoes, as small as you can find

12 large fresh basil leaves, torn into small pieces

olive oil

300g pasta bows (or any shaped pasta)

knob of butter

The 4-year cycle: Juvenile scallops are bought from growers and put into lantern nets. After a period of time they are removed and are scattered on the seabed, like sowing a field with seeds. They remain on the seabed for two years until they mature and are ready for picking. Commercial divers hand pick healthy, correct sized scallops, leaving any that are not big enough undisturbed. This 4-year cycle allows the scallops to reproduce twice, thus keeping the numbers at a sustainable level.

Marco and Ernesto D'Agostino

Hamiltons
4 -5 Brunswick Terrace
Weymouth
DT4 7RW

Tel: 01305 789544

Symphony of Fish

Mr and Mrs Barth

Jaspers Restaurant
57 Hogshill Street
Beaminster
DT8 3AG

Tel: 01308 862600

Ingredients

100g smoked halibut fillet

200g salmon fillet

200g cod or bream fillet

For garnish: 4 cooked prawns and mussels

The Sauce:
3 tbsp fish stock

3 tbsp dry white wine

2 finely chopped shallots

2 tbsp double cream

200g very cold butter (cut into small pieces)

salt and pepper

Serves 1 or 2

Method

1. Gently poach all the fish in fish stock

2. In a small heavy saucepan heat the wine and shallots until almost dry. Add the cream and continue boiling until the mixture is reduced to 1 - 2 tbsp glacé

3. On a low heat gradually whisk in the butter taking the pan on and off the heat so the butter melts creamily to form a light sauce. The mixture should be whisked continually so that the butter forms an emulsion as it melts. At this point you can either strain the shallots out of the mixture or leave them in

To serve: pile the fish up on a warm plate and surround with the sauce. Garnish with the prawns and mussels.

Fishing off Dorset targets a wide variety of catches from crabs and lobsters caught using pots, finfish such as bass, cod and plaice caught by trawling or using lines, to scallops that are either dredged or handpicked.

Trout Cleopatra

Jaspers Restaurant

Method

1. Coat the trout in the seasoned flour and cook in the butter
2. Repeat with the roes. Keep both warm
3. To make the sauce place the wine and vermouth in a small heavy pan and boil until it is reduced by a half
4. Add the cream and keep boiling until there is only about 3 - 4 tbsp of mixture left
5. On a low heat gradually add the butter whisking continuously, the pan must be lifted off the heat every few seconds so that the butter melts creamily to form a light sauce
6. Add the prawns and capers and season with salt and pepper

To serve: arrange the fish an roes on a warm plate and surround with the sauce, garnish with parsley sprigs.

Ingredients

2 trout

100g prawns

1 tsp capers

4 soft roes

knob of butter

flour

parsley to garnish

The Sauce:
125ml dry white wine

125ml dry white vermouth

2 tbsp double cream

200g very cold unsalted butter (cut into small pieces)

salt and pepper

Serves 2

Ingredients

2 tbsp butter

2 tbsp flour

145ml milk

145ml single cream

450g mullet poached and removed from the bone

100g sliced mushrooms

4 spring onions, finely chopped

salt and freshly ground black pepper

3 tbsp of grated strong cheddar cheese

3 tbsp of breadcrumbs

1 lemon

Serves 2

Fleet Mullet

Method

1. Melt the butter in a small pan, add the flour and cook for 1 minute. Gradually add the milk and finally the cream

2. Add the poached fish, sliced mushrooms, the white part of the spring onions and season with salt and pepper

3. Divide between 4 scallop shells or dishes

4. Mix the breadcrumbs and the grated cheese together and sprinkle on top of the fish mixture. Bake for 25 minutes at 200°C, 400°F or gas mark 6

Spawning and nursery areas:

Dorset waters provide significant spawning and nursery areas for many different species and it is important that they are kept healthy so that fish stocks can be replenished. Poole Harbour and the Fleet are designated bass nursery areas which means that restrictions apply to how fish might be caught.

Stuffed Fleet Mullet

Liz Moxham

Method

1. De-scale, gut and clean the fish
2. Mix all the remaining ingredients, except the wine, in a bowl until it is a firm consistency
3. Spoon into the inside of the fish and sew it up with a needle and cotton
4. Put into a large ovenproof dish, dot with butter and pour over 2 glasses of white wine. Cover with foil and cook at 180°C, 350°F or gas mark 4 for 1 to 1$^1/_2$ hours depending on the size of the fish

Ingredients

1 large Fleet mullet

brown breadcrumbs

fresh parsley

grated lemon rind

dried apricots (chopped)

salt and lots of freshly ground black pepper

egg yolk to bind together

white wine

Serves 2

Bass can be caught either using a rod and line or in nets. It is better if a rod and line is used as there is no disturbance of the seabed. It is easy to tell which method has been used because if it has been caught by rod and line the bass will be less marked and will also be a lot firmer.

Pan-fried Mackerel with Mustard Sauce

Bridget Loveday

Ingredients

2 prepared mackerel or 4 fillets

English mustard

flour for coating

sea salt and ground black pepper

worcestershire sauce

olive oil and sesame oil for frying

For the sauce:
300ml fish stock

25g butter

25g flour

cream to enrich the sauce

splash of white wine

I tsp English mustard

fennel - chopped

2 shallots - finely chopped

fresh dill

squeeze of lemon juice

tabasco (optional)

Serves 2

Method

1. Rub English mustard into the skin of the mackerel. Coat the mackerel in seasoned flour and pan fry in olive and sesame oil. While cooking add a splash of worcestershire sauce to the pan for extra flavour

2. Make the sauce by melting the butter in a small pan. Add the flour and cook through for a minute. Add the fish stock, stirring constantly. When thickened add the shallots, fennel, mustard, and wine. Cook through for a few minutes then add the cream, dill, lemon juice and tabasco sauce. Check seasoning

Serve with new potatoes and green salad.

Mackerel

Mackerel are usually caught using hand lines, a method that does not damage the seabed. However, 'Seine nets' are a traditional method of fishing for Mackerel from Chesil beach which is still practiced today. These nets are deployed in a half circle with one end on the beach and the other taken by a special rowing boat (a lerret) into the sea. The net is then moved around a shoal of mackerel and pulled onto the shore. This method is very labour intensive and to transport the fish off the beach involves lots of manpower.

Often the fishermen use birds, such as the terns who are fishing for the whitebait the mackerel are chasing, to locate the shoals of mackerel. This is a traditional fishing method now only practised by a few, that works with nature.

Cheese and Crab Pasty

The Pulpit Inn
Portland Bill
Portland
Tel: 01305 821237

Ingredients

75g soft butter

150g plain flour

50g mature grated cheddar

$1/2$ tsp mustard powder

pinch of cayenne pepper

1 large beaten egg

200g white and brown crabmeat

145ml cheese sauce

Serves 4 - 6

Method

1. Rub the butter into the flour and add the cheese, mustard and cayenne

2. Add enough water to make a smooth dough

3. Cover and leave in the fridge for 20 minutes

4. Roll thinly and cut into 12 rounds to fit into a pattie tin, prick the base and cook for approximately 15-20 minutes at gas mark 4, 350°F or 180°C

5. Cool and remove from tins

6. Mix the crabmeat with the cheese sauce, fill the cooked pasty cases and sprinkle with a little grated cheese

7. Brown under the grill

Serve hot on a bed of lettuce and a wedge of lemon.

Mr Alan Lander -
(almost retired fisherman at Swanage)

Alan says that the way fish and shellfish are caught has changed over the decades. However, one of the earliest fishing methods, is still used today. This is the hand picking of species, such as winkles, cockles and oysters. Oysters were once far more commonplace as a general food rather than the luxury items they have become today. Lobsters and brown crab were caught in traditional "Withy" inkwell type pots, which were hand crafted from willow. Today they are manufactured using non-biodegradable nylon.

Whitefish have always been caught using static nets, a sheet net with floats at the top and lead weights at the bottom which only catch the prime fish, allowing the smaller ones to escape. More recently otter and beam trawls have been developed which are towed behind boats. These are more efficient but less selective.

Preparing seafood

Crab
(illustrated left)

1. Once cooked, twist off the legs and claws and with the crab on its back pull off the belly shell by the eyes
2. Remove all the meat from the belly shell, cracking the shell when you reach a new cavity
3. Remove the small stomach sac and dead men's fingers (gills) from the body shell
4. Remove the meat from the body shell keeping the white and brown meat separate
5. Crack open the claws by gently tapping with a hammer and remove the meat from the claws and legs with a skewer

Mussels

If the mussel is open when raw or shut when cooked do not eat as they will not be fresh

1. Scrape away any barnacles with a knife
2. Pull away the beard
3. Wash and scrub the mussel shells

The flat fish

1. Wash the fish
2. Cut around the head and down the centre of the fish, the knife must reach the backbone through the skin
3. Insert the knife under the flesh at the head end
4. Keeping the knife parallel to the bone slice away the fillet using long sweeping strokes
5. Repeat this process but begin at the tail end of the fish
6. Turn the fish over and repeat the whole process for the other side

You should end up with four fillets

Prawns

1. Hold the body and twist off the head
2. Peel the legs and shell away from the flesh
3. Hold the tail and gently pull out the flesh

Round fish

1. Wash the fish
2. Lift the gill fin and make a diagonal cut behind the head
3. Insert the knife at the head end and, keeping the knife flat, cut along the back of the fish
4. Keeping the knife flat to the bone cut away the fillet from head to tail with short sweeping strokes
5. Turn the fish over and repeat the whole process

You should end up with two fillets

Oysters

1. Using an oyster knife push the tip of the blade through the edge of the top hinge, when it snaps pull up the top shell leaving the juices in the bottom shell
2. Cut through the muscle attached to the top shell and discard the top shell
3. Slide the knife under the oyster to detach the muscle from the bottom shell

Don't wash oysters in water as it diminishes the flavour, always wash in oyster juice

Lobster
(illustrated right)

1. Once cooked, pull off the claws
2. Cut the lobster in half down the centre using a knife
3. Remove the stomach sac, intestine and liver and then remove all the meat
4. Crack open the claws and legs (optional) with a hammer
5. Remove the translucent bone and the meat from the claws and legs

Scallops

Do not use any scallops that are already open as they are dead and may not be fresh

1. Insert a knife between the shells near the hinge muscle and pull sharply to break
2. Snap off and discard the flat shell
3. Insert a knife under the skirt and lift off, discard the skirt and black innards, which leaves the muscles
4. Wash the scallop

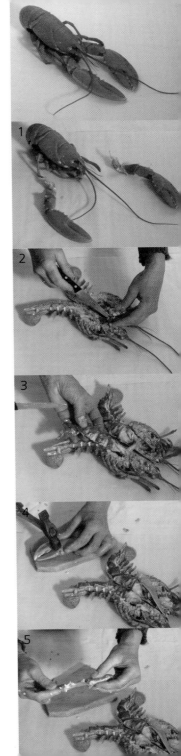

Contributing to this book

Bridget Loveday

Editor

Bridget is the Marine Conservation Officer at the Dorset Wildlife Trust. She started her first career in the food industry but after travelling for three years returned to Britain and retrained in Environmental Management at the University of Northumbria. She came up with the idea of producing a conservation seafood cookbook and got the full support of the Dorset Joint Marine Committee to carry it through.

Maisie Hill

Photographer

Maisie grew up in London. She got involved in photography at 18, spending hours taking pictures and developing them in her dark room. Always having her camera with her has given Maisie enough experience to take on various projects such as Lyme Regis carnival, fashion shoots and family portraits. She has exhibited her work in Bristol and London. Maisie moved to Lyme Regis, Dorset fifteen years ago and has two young daughters.

She continues to increase her photography experience and has spent a great deal of time, effort and expertise in producing the food and fishing photographs for this book.

Ann Gray

Illustrator

Ann grew up in rural Kent, where she became fascinated by nature. She moved to the United States of America where she lived and worked for eighteen years. She has worked at the Natural History Museum of Harvard University and also as a volunteer at the Massachusetts Audubon Conservation Society where she cared for wildlife, developed art and educational projects and illustrated for their magazine. Ann attended the Art Institute of Boston, specialising in Nature Illustration. Ann now lives in Dorset and through her passion and flair for wildlife has produced the wonderful illustrations featured throughout this book.

Sue Tinkler

Graphic Designer

Sue has been working as a designer for sixteen years. She started work in London, then moved to Hampshire ten years ago. Among other things, Sue designs countryside interpretation, trail guides and other environmental related publications. Sue designed this book.

Dr. Ken Collins

Photographer

Ken is a Senior Research Fellow at the School of Oceanography, University of Southampton. He is a member of the Dorset Joint Marine Committee and has marine projects both at home and abroad. He is an experienced diver and has been diving Dorset's waters for over thirty years.
He has contributed some outstanding marine photographs to this book.

Richard Edmonds

Photographer

Richard's interest in the natural world started from collecting fossils on Charmouth beach. He is a keen diver and has been diving and taking pictures for the past 10 years - mostly off the Dorset coast. His favourite dive site is the wreck of the Baygitano off Lyme Regis.

Richard has provided some of the excellent marine wildlife photographs for this book.

Location map

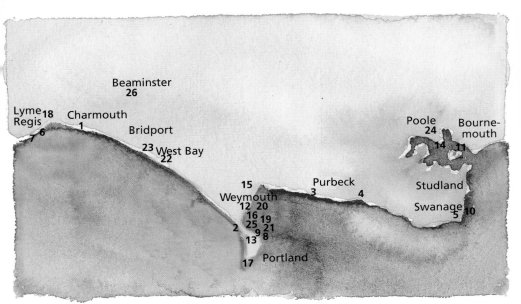

Beaminster
26

Lyme **18** Charmouth
Regis **1**
7 6
Bridport
23 West Bay
22

15 Purbeck
Weymouth **3** **4**
12 20
16 19
2 25 21
9 8
13
17 Portland

Poole Bourne-
24 mouth
14 11

Studland
Swanage
5 10

Marine Conservation Centres

1. Charmouth Heritage Coast Centre
   01297 560772

2. Chesil and the Fleet Nature Reserve Centre
   01305 760579

3. Lulworth Heritage Centre
   01929 400587

4. Purbeck Marine Wildlife Reserve, Kimmeridge
   01929 481044

5. Durlston Marine Project, Durlston Country Park
   01929 421111

Fishing Fleets

6. Lyme Regis
7. Lyme Bay
8. Weymouth
9. Portland
10. Durlston Head
11. Poole

Fishing Ports

12. Weymouth
13. Portland
14. Poole

Restaurants

15. Hamiltons
16. Perrys
17. The Pulpit
18. Polly Victoria
19. Mallams at the Quay
20. The Sea Cow
21. Floods
22. Marsh Barn
23. Riverside
24. Storm Fish
25. Abbotsbury Oyster Farm
26. Jaspers

This project is sponsored by:

Dorset County Council

Dorset County Council has an established national and European reputation in the field of integrated coastal zone management. It initiated the Dorset Coast Forum in 1995 and it continues to provide its secretariat. The County Council were the lead agency in the partnership which funded the production of the Dorset Coast Strategy which recently won a Commendation from the Royal Town Planning Institute for its pioneering approach to the planning and management of coastal zones.

Environment Agency

The Environment Agency's primary role is to protect and improve the environment and contribute to the delivery of sustainable development and the conservation of biodiversity. The Agency is responsible for the protection of wild salmonids (salmon and sea trout) and species which use estuaries eg. bass, sea lamprey and shad. It works closely with local Sea Fishery Committees with regard to the regulation of the local fisheries to prevent over-exploitation.

Weymouth and Portland Borough Council

Fishing has always been an essential part of the life of people in Weymouth and Portland. Fishing has taken place from Weymouth and Portland harbours and historically from Chesil Beach using the Portland lerret. Both Portland Harbour and the fleet are areas where aquaculture occurs. Weymouth and Portland Borough Council are pleased to help sponsor this project and support sustainable fishing in the long term.

The Joint Marine Programme

In June 1997 The Wildlife Trusts and WWF-UK joined forces under the Joint Marine Programme. Their vision is to ensure the conservation of marine wildlife and healthy seas and their goal is to increase effectiveness of both partners in the local, national and international delivery of marine and coastal conservation.

We would also like to thank Mr Julian Francis, a long time member of the Dorset Wildlife Trust, who kindly donated money to help with the sponsorship of this project.